Weight Loss

Recipes

Part I

Breakfast

CONTENTS

Part I:

Breakfast

Recipes

Part I: Breakfast

Mixed Berry Oatmeal

Oatmeal is one of the best breakfast choices that will keep you full for hours. The meal has a very high fiber content at 17 grams compared to regular oatmeal which has a fiber content of 3 grams per serving. The total calorie count is 123 kcal, which is very low and perfect for weight loss. High fiber and low- calorie diets are imperative for weight loss. Further, you can use mixed berries and other dried fruit as toppings, which will provide you with additional fiber and anti-oxidants. The recipe is super easy, and it only takes 7 minutes to prepare!

Serving size: 1

Estimated time7 minutes

Ingredients

- 1/3 cup almond milk (unsweetened)
- 1/3 cup oatmeal (All-Bran Bran Buds)
- 1/3 cup water
- I pinch cinnamon
- ½ cup mixed berries
- 1 scoop protein powder (optional)

Instructions

1. Mix oatmeal, almond milk, and cinnamon in a saucepan and place over medium heat for 3 minutes. Stir occasionally and ensure that it is not sticking at the bottom.

2. Add water and leave to simmer. Keep stirring every few minutes until all the water has been absorbed and a thick consistency has formed. This should take around 4 minutes.

3. In case it is too thick for you, add water or almond milk and stir.

4. Remove from heat and serve.

5. Add blueberries, strawberries, red berries or any other toppings of your choice. Since you are on a weight loss quest, avoid honey and other sugary additives such as maple syrup.

6.   Enjoy while it is still warm.

Nutritional Value per Serving

Calories: 123 Kcal

Protein: 13g

Net carbs: 20g

Sugar: 14g

Fat: 3g

Sodium: 347mg

☐

Weight Loss Magic Soup

This soup is a combination of two popular weight loss soups; weight watchers garden vegetable soup and cabbage soup. The key additives which are not in either of the previous recipes are kidney beans and protein powder. The two helps to keep you fuller for longer, and the low-calorie count makes it perfect for weight loss. Even better, the soup is not limited for breakfast but can be suitable for lunch and a snack.

Serving size: 3
Estimated Time: 1 hour

Ingredients

- 5 oz. chicken broth (use low-sodium)
- 4 oz. Italian tomatoes (diced)
- 1 small onion
- 1 clove minced garlic
- 1-ounce mushrooms (sliced)
- 1 carrot (peeled and sliced)
- ¼ zucchini (sliced)
- ½ yellow squash (diced)
- ¼ cup green beans (either fresh or frozen)
- ½ cup cabbage (shredded)
- ½ tbsp. Italian seasoning
- Salt and pepper to taste

Instructions

1.   Spray a large frying pan with cooking spray. Sauté garlic, carrots, onions, and mushrooms. Stir for around 5 minutes and ensure that all parts of the vegetables are well coated.

2.   Take a large pot and combine the sautéed ingredients with the rest of the ingredients.

3.   Cook over medium heat for 30 min-1 hour. Ensure that the vegetables are fork-tender to represent complete cooking.

4.   Remove from heat and serve.

5.   In case you prepared a lot of soup, freeze the remainder in portions. Ideally, frozen soup can last for as long as 3 weeks as long as it is totally frozen.

Nutritional value per serving

Calories: 57Kcal

Carbohydrates: 11g

Protein: 4g

Fiber: 3g

Sugar: 4g

Fat: 1g

Calcium: 39mg

Iron: 1.5mg

Vitamin c: 22.9 mg

Keto Pancakes

The keto pancakes are gluten-free with a very low carb content, which aids in weight loss. The pancakes are very easy to make, and all you need to do is ensure that you are using almond/coconut milk and flour as substitutes to the normal flour.

Serving size: 2

Estimated time: 30 minutes

Ingredients

- 3 cups almond/coconut flour
- ½ cup almond/coconut milk
- 1 tbsp. sugar
- 1 tbsp. salt
- Cooking oil
- Cinnamon (optional)

Instructions

1.   In a small bowl, add water, sugar, and salt. Mix well.

2.   Add almond milk and water and whisk thoroughly. The butter should be soft and without clumps. However, make sure that it has a thick consistency to prevent it from falling apart while cooking.

3.   Heat pan over medium heat and put a few drops of oil.

4.   Pour in a little butter and spread it out. The shape and size of the pancake are all dependent on the butter that you pour.

5.   Add a little oil to cook on one side, then flip it over and cook the other side.

6.   Enjoy!

Nutritional value per pancake

calories: 240

Total fat: 17.2g

Cholesterol: 216.9mg

Fiber: 6.5g

Protein: 9.6g

Part I: Breakfast

Sugar-free brownies

This meal is 100% sugar-free while still maintaining its taste. This is a perfect recipe for people who want to lose weight while still eating their favorite snacks. Diabetics can comfortably indulge with no harm to them.

Serving size: 3

Estimated time: 45 min

Ingredients

- ½ cup margarine
- ¾ cup all-purpose flour (use almond flour to make it gluten-free)
- 1/8 tbsp. salt
- 2 eggs
- ¼ cup of unsweetened cocoa powder
- 1 cup granular sucrose sweetener
- ¼ cup skimmed milk

- ½ cup chopped walnuts (optional)
- 1 ounce sugar-free, chocolate fudge flavored instant pudding

Instructions

1. Preheat the oven to 175 degrees Celsius (350 degrees F)

2. Grease and flour an 8*8 inch pan

3. In a small saucepan, melt margarine over medium heat and mix with cocoa. Stir thoroughly until they are completely smooth. It is preferable to add the cocoa while margarine is till overheat so that they can melt more efficiently. Remove from heat and set aside to cool.

4. In a large bowl, beat the eggs until they become frothy and stir in the sucrose sweetener. In another bowl sieve flour and mix with salt. Then, stir them into the egg

mixture.

5. Finally, stir in the ¼ cup of milk and walnuts into the mixture.

6. Pour into the preheated pan and flatten it out.

7. Put in the oven and bake for 25-30 minutes. To test whether they have cooked, insert a toothpick. If it comes out clean, then it is ready.

8. Remove from the oven and prepare the frosting as the dough cools.

9. To make the frosting, mix together sugar-free chocolate pudding and 1 cup of skimmed milk with an electric mixer. The ultimate mixture should be very thick.

10. Spread on the cooled brownies, and then cut them in your desired shapes.

11. Enjoy!

Nutritional value

Calories: 74

Fat: 5.7g

Carbohydrates: 4.5g

Protein: 1.9g

Cholesterol: 15mg

Sodium: 70mg

Images

https://pixabay.com/de/photos/blaubeeren-dessert-fr%C3%BChst%C3%BCck-1576407/

https://pixabay.com/de/photos/nussbaum-goji-beeren-haferflocken-642123/

https://pixabay.com/de/photos/k%C3%BCrbissuppe-suppe-hokkaidosuppe-3645375/

https://pixabay.com/de/photos/lebensmittel-pfannkuchen-fr%C3%BChst%C3%BCck-715541/

https://pixabay.com/de/photos/brownie-dessert-kuchen-s%C3%BC%C3%9F-lecker-548591/

https://pixabay.com/de/photos/brownie-schokoladenkuchen-eis-3042106/

https://pixabay.com/de/photos/pfannkuchen-pancake-dessert-3981760/

https://pixabay.com/de/photos/lebensmittel-suppe-mahlzeit-gesund-4936947/

☐ ☐

Part I: Breakfast